M2A2 BRADLEYS

BY JACK DAVID

BELLWETHER MEDIA · MINNEAPOLIS, MN

Are you ready to take it to the extreme?
Torque books thrust you into the action-packed
world of sports, vehicles, and adventure. These books
may include dirt, smoke, fire, and dangerous stunts.
WARNING: read at your own risk.

Library of Congress Cataloging-in-Publication Data

David, Jack, 1968-
  M2A2 Bradleys / by Jack David.
      p. cm. — (Torque. Military machines)
  Includes bibliographical references and index.
  Summary: "Amazing photography and engaging information explain the technologies and
capabilities of the M2A2 Bradley. Intended for students in grades 3 through 7"—Provided by
publisher.
  ISBN-13: 978-1-60014-261-1 (hbk. : alk. paper)
  ISBN-10: 1-60014-261-3 (hbk. : alk. paper)
 1. M2 Bradley infantry fighting vehicle—Juvenile literature. I. Title.
  UG446.5.D3283 2009
  623.7'475—dc22   2008035636

This edition first published in 2009 by Bellwether Media, Inc.

The photographs in this book are reproduced through the courtesy of the United States Department
of Defense.

Printed in the United States of America.

CONTENTS

THE M2A2 IN ACTION...................4

INFANTRY FIGHTING VEHICLE 8

WEAPONS AND FEATURES 12

M2A2 MISSIONS 18

GLOSSARY 22

TO LEARN MORE 23

INDEX 24

THE M2A2 IN ACTION

A big **diesel** engine rumbles as an M2A2 Bradley rolls over sand and rocks. The Bradley's crew of three is transporting six heavily armed soldiers. The crew's **mission** is to carry the soldiers to a secret meeting place behind enemy lines.

The Bradley's crew spots an enemy tank in the distance. The M2A2's **commander** shouts out orders as the **gunner** takes aim. He fires a powerful anti-tank **missile** at the enemy. The tank is destroyed in a ball of fire. The crew quickly gets moving again. The meeting place is near. Their mission is almost complete.

7

INFANTRY FIGHTING VEHICLE

The M2A2 Bradley is an **infantry fighting vehicle (IFV)**. Its job is to safely carry soldiers and their equipment into battle. The Bradley has light **armor** that can protect it from enemy fire. It has tracks that allow it to roll over almost any surface. It can even float on water with an inflatable **pontoon**.

The soldiers carried in the rear compartment of a Bradley can help out in a fight. They can fire their weapons through six firing ports.

The M2 Bradley series entered United States Army service in 1981. The Army has developed several different models since then. The M2A2 model entered service in 1988. The newer M2A3 was introduced in the year 2000. The similar M3 Bradley models carry more weapons, but fewer soldiers.

The Bradley is named for General Omar Nelson Bradley, an important U.S. Army general during World War II.

WEAPONS AND FEATURES

The M2A2 isn't built to attack, but it has plenty of firepower for defense. Its main weapon is an M242 Bushmaster 25mm **chain gun**. This huge gun can fire up to 200 powerful rounds per minute. The M2A2 also has a smaller **machine gun**, the M240 7.62mm.

The crew of a Bradley also uses anti-tank missiles. The Bradley's missile launcher is loaded with BGM-71 TOW missiles. These missiles pack a lot of punch. They can blast through thick tank armor. Crews can launch them from a distance of more than 2 miles (3.2 kilometers).

M2A2 BRADLEY SPECIFICATIONS:

Primary Function: Lightly armored infantry fighting vehicle

Length: 21 feet, 2 inches (6.5 meters)

Width: 10 feet, 9 inches (3.3 meters)

Height: 11 feet, 10 inches (3.6 meters)

Weight: 50,000 pounds (22,700 kilograms)

Engine: Cummins VTA-903T diesel engine

Range: 250 miles (400 kilometers)

Crew: 3

Sometimes, it's better to hide or escape than it is to fight. The Bradley carries **grenade** launchers that can launch smoke grenades. Thick smoke pours out of these grenades. The smoke hides the Bradley so enemies cannot target it.

M2A2 MISSIONS

The Bradley's mission is to transport troops wherever they need to go. The Bradley can move over water and almost any type of land. Its light armor protects the crew from most small enemy attacks. Its powerful engine can push the Bradley 40 miles (64 kilometers) per hour or more.

★ **FAST FACT** ★

The Bradley has a special air filter to protect the crew from poison gas attacks.

Each Bradley has three crew members. The commander is in charge of the mission. The driver looks through the vision port and steers the Bradley. The gunner loads and fires the weapons. The crew works together to quickly get soldiers to the battlefield and bring them home safely.

GLOSSARY

armor—protective plating made of metal or ceramic materials

chain gun—a large gun or cannon that can rapidly fire heavy rounds

commander—the crew member in charge of an M2A2 Bradley

diesel—a type of fuel made from oil, commonly used to power large vehicles

grenade—a small explosive that can be thrown or launched with a grenade launcher

gunner—the Bradley crew member in charge of loading and firing weapons

infantry fighting vehicle (IFV)—an armored vehicle designed to carry troops into battle

machine gun—an automatic weapon that can rapidly fire bullets

missile—an explosive launched at targets on the ground or in the air

mission—a military task

pontoon—a floating platform

TO LEARN MORE

AT THE LIBRARY

Baker, David. *M2A2 Bradley Fighting Vehicle*. Vero Beach, Fla.: Rourke, 2007.

David, Jack. *United States Army*. Minneapolis, Minn.: Bellwether, 2008.

Green, Michael. *Infantry Fighting Vehicles: the M2A2 Bradleys*. Mankato, Minn.: Capstone, 2004.

ON THE WEB

Learning more about military machines is as easy as 1, 2, 3.

1. Go to www.factsurfer.com.

2. Enter "military machines" into the search box.

3. Click the "Surf" button and you will see a list of related Web sites.

With factsurfer.com, finding more information is just a click away.

INDEX

1981, 10
1988, 10
2000, 10
air filter, 19
armor, 8, 15, 18
BGM-71 TOW missiles, 15
Bradley, General Omar
  Nelson 11
commander, 6, 21
crew, 4, 6, 15, 18, 21
diesel engine, 4, 18
driver, 21
firing ports, 9
grenade launchers, 17
gunner, 6, 21
infantry fighting vehicle
  (IFV), 8
M240 7.62mm machine
  gun, 12

M242 Bushmaster 25mm
  chain gun, 12
M2A3 Bradley, 10
M3 Bradley, 10
missiles, 6, 15
missions, 4, 6, 18, 21
poison gas, 19
pontoon, 8
smoke grenades, 17
soldiers, 4, 8, 9, 10, 21
tracks, 8
United States Army, 10, 11
World War II, 11